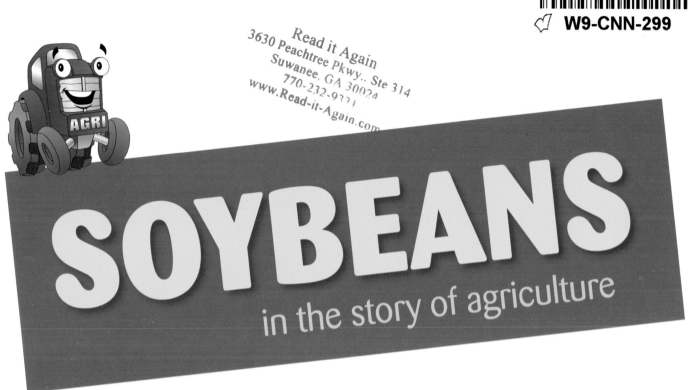

SOYBEANS
in the story of agriculture

Susan Anderson & JoAnne Buggey

Book design by Nancy Roberts

Northwest Arm Press

Hello!

I'm Agri-Culture, Agri for short.

I'm here to introduce **soybeans,** an important agricultural product.

We will see soybeans in all five parts of agriculture:

production ⟩ processing ⟩ distribution ⟩ marketing ⟩ consumerism ⟩

Let's go!

Chapter 1 • The **production** of soybeans

Agricultural production is growing crops or raising animals.

production	processing	distribution	marketing	consumerism

- seeds and plants
- farming
- harvesting and storage

This is a **soybean.** It is also the soybean seed.

It's a fact!

The outside of the soybean is called the hull.
The brown or black spot is called the
hilum (HY lum). This is where the seed was
attached to the pod. Soybeans may be round
or oval. Most of the soybeans grown in the
United States are beige. They also come in
brown, black, speckled, yellow, or green.

Did you know?

Soybeans have been
grown and used in China
for many centuries. They
were brought to the
United States in the late
1700s. Benjamin Franklin
is said to have sent
soybeans from England to
the United States.

These are **soybean plants.**

Did you know?

Soybean plants appear within 2 weeks after seeds are planted. In 4 to 6 weeks they flower, usually in pink, purple, or white. In another 2 weeks pods grow where the flowers were. It then takes another 6 to 8 weeks before the pods are ready to harvest. From planting to harvest soybeans take about 14 to 18 weeks.

It's a fact!

Soybeans are a legume (LEG yoom). Peas, beans, and peanuts are also legumes. The fruit of legumes grows in pods. Soybean pods usually contain 2 to 4 seeds. One soybean plant averages 20 to 30 pods.

Soybeans grow on **farms.**

Did you know?

Soybean farmers work all year long.

Spring
- Prepare the soil
- Plant seeds

Summer
- Control weeds
- Control insects
- Irrigate where necessary

Fall
- Harvest
- Store beans
- Work the soil

Winter
- Market the crop
- Order seeds
- Take care of machinery

It's a fact!

Soybeans are a renewable resource – that means farmers can grow a new crop every year.

It is **spring.** This farmer is filling his planter with soybeans.

Did you know?

Most soybean farmers do not plant soybeans on the same field two years in a row. This is called crop rotation. It helps farmers grow healthy soybean plants and it is better for the soil. Farmers are concerned about the environment.

It's a fact!

The United States is one of the leading soybean producers in the world.

Now it is **summer.**

This is a field of soybeans that has been growing for about two months.
The soybean pods are forming where the flowers were.

It's a fact!

For a good soybean crop adequate water is needed during the growing season. If there is not enough rainfall, some farmers use irrigation to provide water.

Did you know?

William Morse is called the Father of Soybeans in America. In the early 1900s he brought about 4,500 varieties of soybeans from Asia to the United States. He believed that soybeans would become one of America's major crops.

Fall has come.

A combine is used to harvest soybeans. It cuts the soybean plants, separates the beans from the pods, and cleans the soybeans so that no bits of pod or stem are poured into the cart nearby.

Did you know?

Soybean plants grow to be about three feet tall. In the fall the plants stop growing and become dry. Then the leaves turn yellow and drop to the ground. The pods turn a golden tan and are ready to be harvested.

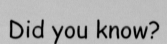

It's a fact!

Before the combine was invented harvesting was done with reapers and threshers. In 1835 Hiram Moore invented the combine. It could do the work of both the reaper and the thresher. It was nearly 100 years before these combines became widely used.

These round **storage** bins hold soybeans brought from farms. This truck is waiting to be loaded with soybeans that will be delivered to a processing plant.

It's a fact!

Most soybeans grown in the United States go to processing.

Did you know?

After being harvested the soybeans are stored on farms or taken to large storage areas in nearby communities. These storage areas are called elevators.

Chapter 2 • The **processing** of soybeans

Processing is making crops or animals into products you can eat or use.

| production | processing | distribution | marketing | consumerism |

- basic steps
- specific products

Most soybeans are **processed** in a plant like this. Their hulls are removed and the beans are crushed and rolled into flakes.

Did you know?

The first flakes made by crushing soybeans are full-fat or oil flakes. The oil flakes are separated into white, defatted flakes and crude oil.

Hulls

Oil Flakes

White Flakes

Crude Oil

These are some of the **products** made from hulls, defatted flakes, and crude oil. Later, they can be made into or used in products like animal feed, biodiesel, and ink.

Pelleted Hulls

Soybean Meal

REFINED & BLEACHED OIL

Did you know?

Soybean oil is stored in tanks like the white one.
Soybean meal is stored in bins like the gray ones.

Farm animals are among the biggest consumers of **soybean meal** in the United States.

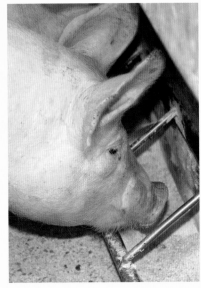

Did you know?

Soybean meal contains high-quality protein which helps farmers raise healthy animals. About 80% of United States soybean meal is fed to farm animals including chickens, pigs, cattle, and turkeys.

It's a fact!

Soybean meal is also used in food for pets, zoo animals, and fish.

Biodiesel is a biofuel manufactured from soybean oil in plants like this.

Did you know?

Biodiesel is the fastest-growing alternative diesel fuel in the United States.

It's a fact!

A bushel of soybeans weighs 60 pounds. The bushel of soybeans can be processed into 79% soybean meal and 18% soybean oil. One bushel of soybeans makes 1½ gallons of biodiesel.

Soy **ink** is valuable to the printing process because it is environmentally friendly.

Did you know?

Soy ink is made from soybean oil. The ink produces bright colors and comes from a renewable resource – soybeans.

It's a fact!

Soy ink is used for printing many United States newspapers.

A variety of **drinks** can be made from soy.

Did you know?

Soy milk is made from whole soybeans. Some people have lactose intolerance or are allergic to dairy foods. Soy products can help many of these people have a balanced diet.

It's a fact!

You could make this soy drink. Ask an adult to help you. Here is the recipe:

Strawberry Banana Smoothie

3 cups vanilla soy milk
1 cup strawberries
1 banana

Mix in blender until smooth. To make it frothy use frozen strawberries. Serves 4.

Even **cloth and fibers** can be made from soy.

Did you know?

After tofu is made from soy milk, the left-over oils can be spun into soft fibers. **SOYSILK®** is one brand name for these fibers made from soy.

It's a fact!

In the 1930s Henry Ford had two suits made of soy.

Bachrach Studios/CORBIS

Chapter 3 • The **distribution** of soybeans

Distribution is delivering a product from where it is produced or grown to the places where it will be used.

production **processing** **distribution** **marketing** **consumerism**

- soybean-producing states
- transportation
- U.S. soybean exports

Soybeans are grown in many **states.**

SEATTLE

Washington

Oregon

Montana

Idaho

Wyoming

OAKLAND

Nevada

Utah

Colorado

California

Arizona

New Mexico

North Dakota

South Dakota

Minnesota

DULUTH

Wisconsin

Iowa

Nebraska

Michigan

Illinois

Indiana

Ohio

Kansas

Missouri

Oklahoma

Arkansas

Kentucky

Tennessee

Texas

Mississippi

Louisiana

Alabama

Georgia

North Carolina

South Carolina

Florida

NEW ORLEANS

Alaska

Hawaii

Vermont

Maine

New Hampshire

Massachusetts

New York

Rhode Island

Connecticut

Pennsylvania

New Jersey

Delaware

West Virginia

Virginia

Maryland

It's a fact!

In the United States, most soybeans are grown in thirty-one states, shown here in color.

Did you know?

There are four major ports from which soybeans are shipped to other countries. They are marked on the map.

Transportation – by truck, train, barge, and ship – is the key to distributing soybeans from soybean-growing areas to the rest of the country or to other countries.

Did you know?

The Mississippi River is an important route for delivering soybeans to the port in New Orleans. Barges provide inexpensive and high-quality transportation over long distances.

Soybeans are a leading United States **export.** Soybeans are loaded onto ships to be delivered to other countries.

Did you know?

About one-third of the soybeans grown in the United States are exported. Most soybeans for export are brought to ports unprocessed. Only a small amount of soybean meal and soybean oil are exported.

Chapter 4 • The marketing of soybeans

Marketing is telling about products so that you will know about them and might buy them.

| production | processing | distribution | marketing | consumerism |

- advertising
- soy-themed clothing
- logos

Advertising helps us to know about different products made with soybeans.

We use Soy Biodiesel in our Midway rides

When It Comes To Cleaner Air... Metro Is Full Of Beans!

It's a fact!

New soy products are being developed almost every day. Advertising agencies could be hired to create ads about these new products and place the ads where people can see them.

Did you know?

Advertising tries to persuade you to buy or use a product or service. Look at this ad about the make-believe cereal called Nubbles. Does the ad make you want to try this product?

Where do I get MY morning smile? It's no secret... NUBBLES. Delicious! With soy protein for all-day energy. NUBBLES is in your grocery store now!

NEW
beangood inc.
Nubbles
Grain 'n' Soy
tasty, protein-rich SOY plus 8 nutritious grains
Food for the Life you Love

We are **influenced** to buy products in many ways. Sometimes ads are actually on clothing.

Did you know?

Fairs and trade shows give people a chance to taste foods made from soybeans. And grocery stores often give out free samples of soyfoods along with recipes that can be prepared using soy products.

It's a fact!

This T-shirt, printed with soy ink, lists an amazing number of products made from soybeans.

Logos help us to recognize soy products. These are some soy logos.

Did you know?

A logo can be used in advertising to help us identify a certain product. It is usually a combination of words and pictures. Companies use logos to develop an image or loyalty to their product.

It's a fact!

Some states have their own soybean logos. Look to see if your state has a soybean logo.

Chapter 5 • Consumerism and soybeans

Consumerism is **you** choosing, buying, and using products.

| production | processing | distribution | marketing | consumerism |

- MyPyramid
- soyfoods
- food labeling
- soy products

Soybeans can count in either the **Protein** or the **Vegetables** section of MyPlate.

Did you know?

Soybeans are a source of high-quality protein and contain all eight of the essential amino acids, just like meat. Very few vegetables have all eight amino acids.

It's a fact!

Soybeans are high in fiber and contain essential vitamins and minerals including calcium, iron, potassium, and folic acid. This makes soybeans a nutritious vegetable. Scientists today are researching the benefits of soy for the body and its role in the prevention of disease.

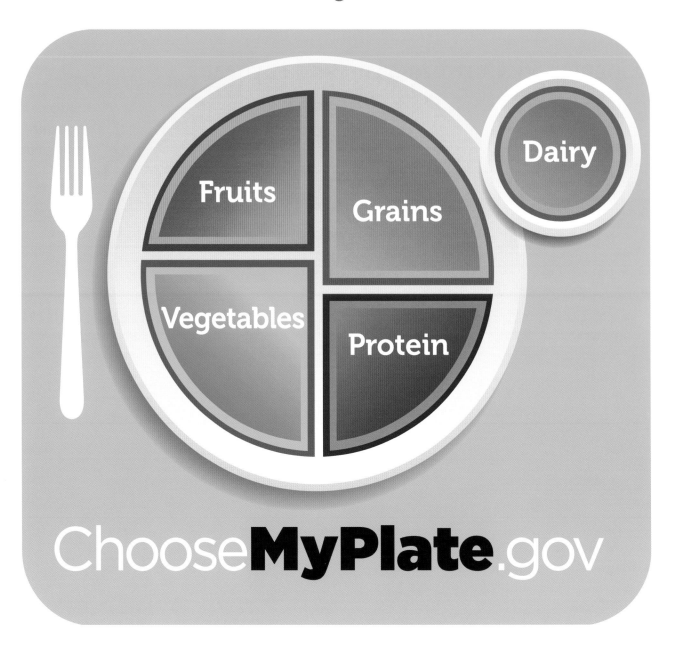

Fruits

Grains

Dairy

Vegetables

Protein

Choose**MyPlate**.gov

Here are some **soyfoods**.

Did you know?

Soybeans are an economical way to make other foods more nutritious. Soy-enriched foods can be found in almost every aisle of the grocery store.

It's a fact!

Tofu is one of the most popular ways of eating soybeans around the world.
Tofu is
• cholesterol-free
• low in sodium
• high in protein
• low in saturated fat
• a source of calcium

These are some of the ways we **eat** soybeans. Point to any of these you have eaten.

Did you know?

The average American consumes nearly half a cup of soybeans in some form each day. But soyfoods are eaten much more in other parts of the world.

It's a fact!

Edamame (ed uh ma may) is a Japanese dish made from green soybeans. The beans can usually be found in the freezer section of the grocery store. Ask an adult to help you prepare edamame.

Edamame

Boil the beans in the pod for five minutes.
Sprinkle them with a bit of salt.
Allow them to cool so you can handle them.
Open the pods and eat the soybeans inside.

These are some of the other ways we use **soy products.**

It's a fact!

Soy candles last a
long time and burn
very cleanly.

Did you know?

Over 2,000 crayons can
be made from one bushel
of soybeans.

BAR-B-Q GRILL CLEANER

Soy Wax Blend

Soybeans are an important part of our lives. Maybe **you** will play a role in the future of soybeans.

Soybean Activities

The next time you go to the grocery store look for soy products you could buy.

- Write your own story about each chapter.

- Make a collection of soy ads and logos from newspapers and magazines.

- Divide a page of paper into four parts and draw a picture in each part showing something you learned about soybeans.

- Look at your school lunches for soy products.

- List soybean products you have tasted.

- Taste a soybean product you haven't tried before.

Make the recipes on page 17 and page 30.

next page…Soybean in a Bag!

Soybean in a Bag

You will need a paper punch,
a small jeweler's bag,
36" yarn, 2 soybean seeds,
and 1 cotton ball.

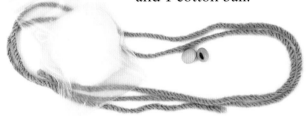

1. Punch a hole in the top of the bag.
2. Dip the cotton ball in water and give it three flat squeezes to wring out excess moisture.
3. Place the moistened cotton ball inside the bag.
4. Place two soybean seeds in the bag, one on each side of the dampened cotton ball.
5. Seal the baggie or leave it open – that becomes part of your experiment.
6. Thread the yarn through the hole punched in the bag and tie the ends.
7. Place the Soybean in a Bag around your neck like a necklace. Wear it outside your shirt or tucked inside. Again that becomes part of your experiment.

8. The soybean should soon swell up from the moisture and germination should take place in about three days. Once one soybean has germinated, remove the other one from the bag.
9. Eventually you can cut off the bottom of the bag, remove the tiny plant along with the cotton ball, and transplant it into soil.

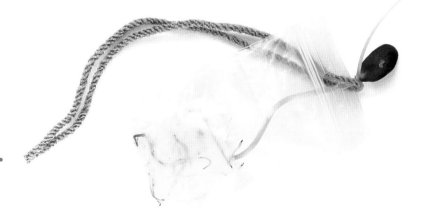

The Story of Agriculture series

SOYBEANS in the Story of Agriculture
American Farm Bureau Federation
2010 Book of the Year

PIGS & PORK in the Story of Agriculture

forthcoming...
  Corn, 2011
  Beef
  Wheat
  Dairy
  Poultry

**For children ages 5–8, see the
Awesome Agriculture A-to-Z books:**

SOYBEANS, an A-to-Z book
American Farm Bureau Federation
2010 PreK-K Accurate Ag Book

PIGS, an A-to-Z book

CORN, an A-to-Z book

forthcoming...
  Beef
  Wheat
  Dairy
  Poultry

Soybeans in the Story of Agriculture is also
Minnesota Farm Bureau 2010 Book of the Year.
Both soybean books are also Illinois Ag in the
Classroom 2010 Ag Week Books of the Year.

www.northwestarmpress.com

The Authors

JoAnne Buggey has a PhD in Curriculum & Instruction from the University of Washington (1971). She taught future elementary teachers in the College of Education and Human Development at the University of Minnesota. JoAnne has written dozens of textbooks for children including an American history text, *America! America!* and a civics text, *Civics for Americans.* Her recent multimedia projects include Exploring Where and Why, a program on maps and mapping for grades K–3.

Susan Anderson earned her MS in Curriculum & Instruction from Minnesota State University, Mankato (1988). She is an Education Specialist for University of Minnesota Extension and the College of Food, Agricultural and Natural Resource Sciences. Susan grew up on a farm and lives on a working farm today. During her elementary teaching years she developed an interdisciplinary fifth-grade curriculum to increase agricultural literacy.

Both authors have been elementary teachers in the Minneapolis Public Schools. They currently work with the K-12 Education Program at the University of Minnesota Southwest Research and Outreach Center at Lamberton. They provide workshops for future and current elementary teachers in agricultural literacy. Both have contributed to curriculum projects including materials related to dairy and pigs. The authors serve on various boards related to agriculture and have won awards for quality teaching about agriculture. JoAnne and Susan are currently part of an Improving Teacher Quality grant team.

Acknowledgements

For invaluable assistance, our thanks to Naomi Mortensen and Sam Ziegler at Minnesota Soybean Research & Promotion Council; Robert Anderson, Minnesota soybean producer and farm financial manager; Charles Hall, Beth Holleman, and Laura Rogers at North Carolina Soybean Producers Association; Betty Fyler, South Dakota Research & Promotion Council; Jaime M. Vincent, Kentucky Soybean Association & Promotion Board; Jeff Helms, Alabama Farmers Federation; Abby L. Stutsman, Osborn & Barr; Brett Trout; and Angela McCarthy.

• •

This book is dedicated to Bob

• •

Northwest Arm Press, Inc.
1004-1545 South Park Street
Halifax Nova Scotia Canada B3J 4B3
northwestarmpress.com

Fact-checking and proofreading: Paddy Muir
Project photographer: Lisa Marie Noseworthy, LMNO Photo
Tractor illustrations by Gerry Cleary,
        from an original idea by James Jahoda
Soybean in a Bag based on Soy Boy project, Ag in the
        Classroom

Models:
16: Cohen Anthony Haines Dowden
24: Nicholine Davis
35: Cassidy McCarthy

This product conforms to CPSIA 2011.
Printed in China
Second printing

Library and Archives Canada Cataloguing in Publication

Anderson, Susan, 1950-
    Soybeans in the story of agriculture / Susan Anderson &
JoAnne Buggey.

(Awesome agriculture for kids)
ISBN 978-0-9811335-2-2

    1. Soybean--Juvenile literature. 2. Soybean products--
Juvenile literature.
I. Buggey, JoAnne II. Title. III. Series: Awesome agriculture
for kids

SB205.S7A533 2009   j633.3'4   C2009-901112-3

Image Credits

Cover: David L. Hansen, *Food for Thought, a Geography of Minnesota
    Agriculture in Photos,* University of Minnesota
4: courtesy of Minnesota Soybean Research & Promotion Council
    (MSRPC)
5–6: United Soybean Board (USB)
7: © Bryan Eastham, 2009, used under license from Shutterstock.com
8–10: USB
12–13: USB
14: farm animals, USB; hamster, © Anna Karwowska, 2009, used under
    license from Shutterstock.com
15: plant, SoyMor Biodiesel, LLC, courtesy of MSRPC; pump, USB
16: printer and inks, USB; newspapers, LMNO Photo
17: boy and blender, LMNO Photo; soy milk, USB
18: Ford, Bachrach Studios © Schenectady Museum, Hall of Electrical
    History Foundation/CORBIS; shirts and yarn, LMNO Photo;
    Soysilk® logo courtesy of South West Trading Company, Inc.
20: © Mirec, 2009, used under license from Shutterstock.com
21: train and barge cover, USB courtesy of MSRPC; barges © David
    Gilder, 2009, used under license from Shutterstock.com
22: USB
24: banner © Beth Holleman, used with permission; bus, USB courtesy
    of MSRPC; mock ad, image LMNO Photo and digital composition
    Nancy Roberts Design
25: trade show, USB courtesy of MSRPC; sleeve, John Driemen; cap,
    USB; shirt, LMNO Photo
26: tag, LMNO Photo; biodiesel logo © National Biodiesel Board,
    courtesy of Brett Trout; Soysilk® and Soysilk® Pals logos courtesy
    of South West Trading Company, Inc.; SoySeal, American
    Soybean Association courtesy of MSRPC; Kentucky logo courtesy
    of Kentucky Soybean Association & Promotion Board; Alabama
    logo courtesy of Alabama Farmers Federation
28: United States Department of Agriculture. USDA does not endorse
    any products, services, or organizations.
29: LMNO Photo
30: cookies courtesy of South Dakota Soybean Research and
    Promotion Council (SDSRPC); cheese, USB courtesy of MSRPC;
    salad, SDSRPC; bread, tofu, and edamame, LMNO Photo
31: grill cleaner, USB; all others LMNO Photo
32: person at trade show, USB courtesy of MSRPC; remainder, USB
33: grocery store © Monkey Business Images, 2009, used under license
    from Shutterstock.com; foods, LMNO Photo
34: LMNO Photo
Back cover: see credits for pages 24, 22, and 18.

Every effort has been made to credit copyright holders of images
reproduced in this book. Any omissions will be rectified in subsequent
printings if notice is given to the publisher.